Theo-
logy
&
Life

THEOLOGY AND LIFE SERIES

1. Infallibility: The Crossroads of Doctrine
   by Peter Chirico, S.S.
2. Sacramental Realism: A General Theory of the Sacraments
   by Colman O'Neill, O.P.
3. The Making of Disciples: Tasks of Moral Theology
   by Enda McDonagh
4. Life and Sacrament: Reflections on the Catholic Vision
   by Bishop Donal Murray
5. The Bishop of Rome *by J.M.R. Tillard, O.P.*
6. A Theology for Ministry *by George H. Tavard*
7. Luther and His Spiritual Legacy *by Jared Wicks, S.J.*
8. Vatican II: Open Questions and New Horizons
   Gerald Fagin, S.J., Editor
9. Jesus, The Compassion of God:
   New Perspectives on the Tradition of Christianity
   by Monika K. Hellwig
10. Biblical and Theological Reflections on
    THE CHALLENGE OF PEACE
    John T. Pawlikowski, O.S.M., and
    Donald Senior, C.P., Editors
11. Saints and Sinners in the Early Church: Differing and
    Conflicting Traditions in the First Six Centuries
    by W.H.C. Frend
12. Story Theology *by Terrence Tilley*
13. The Bishop in the Church: Patristic Texts on the Role of the
    Episkopos by Agnes Cunningham, S.S.C.M.
14. Our Eucharistic Prayers in Worship, Preaching and Study
    by Raymond Moloney, S.J.

Other Titles in Preparation

THE BISHOP
IN
THE CHURCH

Patristic Texts
on
The Role of the *Episkopos*

by

Agnes Cunningham, S.S.C.M.

Michael Glazier
Wilmington, Delaware

ABOUT THE AUTHOR

Agnes Cunningham, S.S.C.M., theologian and patristic scholar, is Professor of Patrology and Director of the Department of Church History at Saint Mary of the Lake Seminary in Mundelein, Illinois. She is past president of the Catholic Theological Society of America (1977-1978), and is currently on the Board of Directors of Sacred Heart School of Theology (Hales Corners, Wisconsin) and of *Contemplative Review*. She is theological consultant to the NCCB Ad Hoc Committee on Women in Society and the Church. Among her recent publications is *Prayer: Personal and Liturgical,* Volume 16 of the *Message of the Fathers of the Church.*

✠

First published in 1985 by Michael Glazier, Inc., 1723 Delaware Avenue, Wilmington, DE 19806 • ©1985 by Michael Glazier. All rights reserved • Library of Congress Card Catalog Number 84-73563 • International Standard Book Numbers: Theology and Life Series: 0-89453-295-2; THE BISHOP: 0-89453-469-6 • Cover design by Lillian Brulc • Printed in the United States of America.

Contents

Foreword 7

Abbreviations 8

1. The Didache or the Teaching of the
   Twelve Apostles 9
2. The First Epistle to the Corinthians
   (I Clement) 10
3. Saint Ignatius of Antioch 11
4. The Shepherd of Hermas 20
5. Irenaeus of Lyons 21
6. Clement of Alexandria 24
7. Hippolytus of Rome 25
8. Origen 27
9. Cyprian of Carthage 28
10. Constitutions of the Holy Apostles 38
11. Hilary of Poitiers 40
12. Saint Ambrose 41
13. Saint Jerome 43
14. Saint Augustine of Hippo 45
15. Palladius 47
16. Saint Leo the Great 48
17. Julianus Pomerius 49
18. Saint Caesarius of Arles 51

Bibliography of Works Consulted 60

✤ ❖ ✤

This volume is dedicated to the following bishops who have, in a particular way, supported and encouraged my service in the Church —

Joseph Cardinal Bernardin, Archbishop of Chicago
George Cardinal Flahiff, Retired Archbishop of Winnipeg
Archbishop Thomas C. Kelly, O.P. (Louisville)
Archbishop Bernard F. Law (Boston)
Archbishop Kevin McNamara (Dublin)
Bishop James P. Keleher and Bishop Thomas J. Murphy
former Rectors, Saint Mary of the Lake Seminary
Bishop Wilton D. Gregory
a former student at Saint Mary of the Lake Seminary
Bishop Joseph L. Imesch (Joliet)
Bishop Robert F. Morneau (Auxiliary, Green Bay)
Bishop Michael F. McAuliffe (Jefferson City)
Bishop Arthur J. O'Neill (Rockford)
Bishop Stanley J. Ott (Baton Rouge)
Bishop Daniel L. Ryan (Springfield, IL)
Bishop Ernest L. Unterkoefler (Charleston)
Bishop Austin B. Vaughan (Auxiliary, New York)

✤

Foreword

This collection of sayings of the early Church Fathers on the role of the bishop was begun in response to a request from His Eminence, John Cardinal Cody, late Archbishop of Chicago (1965-1982).

The presentation of these texts in chronological order allows us to discern and follow a development of patristic thought from Clement of Rome (c. A.D. 97) through Caesarius of Arles (A.D. 470-A.D. 543). Here, we can find admonitions to the faithful regarding the respect and obedience due to the bishop along with admonitions to the bishops, themselves. The tone is, at times, exhortatory; at other times, encouraging, even comforting. In many instances, we have the words of bishops addressing other bishops or sharing their personal reflections on the responsibilities of the episcopal ministry.

I am grateful to Michael Glazier who was willing to make this material available to a wider audience than my possibilities allowed.

Agnes Cunningham, S.S.C.M.

Abbreviations

ACW	Ancient Christian Writers
ANF	Ante—Nicene Fathers
ANCL	Ante-Nicene Christian Library
FOTC	Fathers of the Church

The Didache or The Teaching of the Twelve Apostles

This document is one of the most important in early Christian literature. Its origin is dated, uncertainly, between A.D. 60 and A.D. 90. It seems to have been a work used for the instruction of catechumens.

Accordingly, elect for yourselves bishops and deacons, men who are an honor to the Lord, of gentle disposition, not attached to money, honest and well-tried; for they, too, render you the sacred service of the prophets and teachers. Do not, then, despise them; after all, they are your dignitaries together with the prophets and teachers. (*Chapter 15, ACW6.*)

2

The First Epistle to the Corinthians (I Clement)

St. Clement of Rome was one of the successors to St. Peter in the Church of Rome between A.D. 92 and A.D. 101. In his letter to the Church of Corinth, Clement recalls the order which exists in the various offices and ministries of the Church. He speaks here of bishops, priests, and deacons in the vocabulary of the Old Testament.

Special functions are assigned to the high priest; a special office is imposed upon the priests; and special ministrations fall to the Levites. The layman is bound by the rules laid down for the laity. (*40:5, ACW1.*)

3

Saint Ignatius of Antioch

Ignatius was bishop of Antioch in Syria at the beginning of the second century of the Christian Era. He was a great Christian and an outstanding pastor. Ignatius was martyred about the year A.D. 110. We know him through the seven letters he wrote en route to Rome where he was put to death.

In the letters to the churches in Ephesus, Magnesia, Tralles, Philadelphia, and Smyrna, he instructs the Christians on the role of the bishop. In his letter to the young episkopos, *Polycarp, he gives counsel regarding the responsibilities of one who is chief pastor of a particular Church.*

It is therefore proper in every way to glorify Jesus Christ who has glorified you, so that you, fully trained in unanimous submission, may be submissive to the bishop and the presbytery, and thus be sanctified in every respect. (*Ephesians 2:2, ACW 1.*)

Surely , Jesus Christ, our inseparable life, for His part is the mind of the Father, just as the bishops, though appointed throughout the vast, wide earth, represent for their part the mind of Jesus Christ. (*Ephesians 3:2, ACW 1.*)

Hence it is proper for you to act in agreement with the mind of the bishop; and this you do. Certain it is that your presbytery, which is a credit to its name, is a credit to God; for it harmonizes with the bishop as completely as the strings with a harp. This is why in the symphony of your concord and love the praises of Jesus Christ are sung. (*Ephesians 4:1, ACW 1.*)

Assuredly, if the prayer of one or two has such efficacy, how much more that of the bishop and the entire Church! ... Let us take care, therefore, not to oppose the bishop, that we may be submissive to God. (*Ephesians 5:2, 3, ACW 1.*)

... [T]he more anyone observes that a bishop is discreetly silent, the more he should stand in fear of him. Obviously, anyone whom the Master of the household puts in charge of His domestic affairs, ought to be received by us in the same spirit as He who has charged him with this duty. Plainly, then, one should look upon the bishop as upon the Lord Himself. (*Ephesians 6:1, ACW 1.*)

[I]t is fitting not to take advantage of the bishop's youth, but rather, because he embodies the authority of God the Father, to show him every mark of respect.... [T]herefore defer to him — or rather, not to him, but to the Father of Jesus Christ, the bishop of all men. (*Magnesians 3:1, ACW 1.*)

The proper thing, then, is not merely to be styled Christians, but also to be such — just as there are those who style a man a bishop, but completely disregard him in their conduct. Such persons do not seem to me to have a good conscience, inasmuch as they do not assemble [for the liturgy] in the fixed order prescribed by him. (*Magnesians 4, ACW 1.*)

I exhort you to strive to do all things in harmony with God: the bishop is to preside in the place of God, while the presbyters are to function as the Council of the Apostles, and the deacons, who are most dear to me, are

entrusted with the ministry of Jesus Christ. . . .
Let there be nothing among you tending to
divide you, but be united with the bishop and
those who preside — serving at once as a pat-
tern and as a lesson of incorruptibility. (*Magnesians 6:1, 2, ACW 1.*)

Just as the Lord, therefore, being one with the
Father, did nothing without Him, either by
Himself or through the Apostles, so neither
must you undertake anything without the
bishop and the presbyters. . . . Come together,
all of you, as to one temple and one altar, to one
Jesus Christ — to Him who came forth from
one Father and yet remained with, and
returned to, one. (*Magnesians 7:1, 2, ACW 1.*)

Be zealous, therefore, to stand squarely on the
decrees of the Lord and the Apostles, *that in all
things whatsoever you may prosper*, in body
and in soul, in faith and in love, in the Son and
the Father and the Spirit, in the beginning and
the end, together with your most reverend
bishop and with your presbytery — that fit-
tingly woven spiritual crown! — and with your
deacons, men of God. (*Magnesians 13:1, ACW
1.*)

Submit to the bishop and to each other's rights, just as did Jesus Christ in the flesh to the Father, and as the Apostles did to Christ and the Father and the Spirit, so that there may be oneness both of flesh and of spirit. (*Magnesians 13:2, ACW 1.*)

Surely, when you submit to the bishop as representing Jesus Christ, it is clear to me that you are not living the life of men, but that of Jesus Christ, who died for us, that through faith in His death you might escape dying. (*Trallians 2:1, ACW 1.*)

It is needful, then — and such is your practice — that you do nothing without your bishop; but be subject also to the presbytery as representing the Apostles of Jesus Christ, our hope, in whom we are expected to live forever. (*Trallians 2:2, ACW 1.*)

... [L]et all respect the deacon as representing Jesus Christ, the bishop as a type of the Father, and the presbyters as God's high council and as the Apostolic College. Apart from these, no church deserves the name. (*Trallians 3:1, ACW 1.*)

15

... [B]eware of such [heretics]! And you will do so if you are not puffed up and cling insepa-rably to God Jesus Christ [sic], to the bishop, and to the precepts of the Apostles. (*Trallians 7:1, ACW 1.*)

He that is inside the sanctuary is pure; he that is outside the sanctuary is not pure. In other words: he that does anything apart from bishop, presbytery, or deacon has no pure con-science. (*Trallians 7:2, ACW 1.*)

It is certainly fitting for you individually, but especially for the presbyters, to give comfort to the bishop in honor of the Father and Jesus Christ and the Apostles. (*Trallians 12:2, ACW 1.*)

Be obedient to the bishop as to the command-ment, and so, too, to the presbytery. And love one another, man for man, with undivided heart. (*Trallians 13:2, ACW 1.*)

Surely, all those that belong to God and Jesus Christ are the very ones that side with the bishop. (*Philadelphians 3:2, ACW 1.*)

... [I]t was the Spirit who kept preaching in these words: "Apart from the bishop do nothing; preserve your persons as shrines of God; cherish unity, shun divisions; do as Jesus Christ did, for He, too, did as the Father did." (*Philadelphians 7:2, ACW 1.*)

Where there is division and passion, there is no place for God. Now, the Lord forgives all if they change their mind and by this change of mind return to union with God and the council of the bishop. (*Philadelphians 8:1, ACW 1.*)

You must all follow the lead of the bishop, as Jesus Christ followed that of the Father; follow the presbytery as you would the Apostles; reverence the deacons as you would God's commandment. (*Smyrnaeans 8:1, ACW 1.*)

Let no one do anything touching the Church, apart from the bishop. (*Smyrnaeans 8:1, ACW 1.*)

Where the bishop appears, there let the people be, just as where Jesus Christ is, there is the Catholic Church. (*Smyrnaeans 8:2, ACW 1.*)

It is not permitted without authorization from the bishop either to baptize or to hold an agape; but whatever he approves is also pleasing to God. (*Smyrnaeans 8:2, ACW 1.*)

✤

It is well to revere God and bishop. He who honors a bishop is honored by God. (*Smyrnaeans 9:1, ACW 1.*)

✤

Do justice to your office with the utmost solicitude, both physical and spiritual. Be concerned about unity, the greatest blessing. (*Polycarp 1:2, ACW 1.*)

✤

Bear with all, just as the Lord does with you. *Have patience with all in charity*, as indeed you do. To prayer give yourself unceasingly; beg for an increase in understanding; watch without letting your spirit flag. Speak to each one singly in imitation of God's way. Bear the infirmities of all, like a master athlete. The greater the toil, the greater the reward. (*Polycarp 1:2, ACW 1.*)

✤

If you love good disciples, you can expect no thanks. Rather, reduce to subjection, by gentleness, the more pestiferous. Not every hurt is healed by the same plaster. (*Polycarp 2:1, ACW 1.*)

As a pilot calls on winds and a storm-tossed mariner looks homeward, so the times call on you to win your way to God. As God's athlete, be sober; the stake is immortality and eternal life. (*Polycarp 2:3, ACW 1.*)

Men that seem worthy of confidence, yet teach strange doctrines, must not upset you. Stand firm, like an anvil under the hammer. It is like a great athlete to take blows and yet win the fight. For God's sake above all we must endure everything, so that God, in turn, may endure us. (*Polycarp 3:1, ACW 1.*)

Nothing must be done without your approval; nor must you do anything without God's approval.... (*Polycarp 4:1, ACW 1.*)

4

The Shepherd of Hermas

The Shepherd is an apocryphal apocalypse authored by Hermas, the brother of St. Pius I (A.D. 140-155). The work is especially important for its teaching on the Sacrament of Reconciliation and on ethical Christian concepts.

Listen now concerning the stones which go into the building. The stones which are square and white and which fit neatly in place, these are the apostles and bishops and teachers and deacons who walked according to the majesty of God and who ministered to the elect of God in holiness and reverence, in the work of overseeing and teaching and in giving service. Some of them have fallen asleep and some are still alive. They always agreed among themselves and had peace among themselves and listened to one another; and that is why in the building of the tower they fit neatly into place. (Vision 3, 5, 1, *The Faith of the Early Fathers*, Volume One.)

Irenaeus of Lyons

St. Irenaeus was second Bishop of Lugdunum (Lyons) in the Christian Church of Gaul. He is the most important theologian of the second century, known both as an anti-heretical writer and as the Father of Catholic theology. He was respected in the Church as a peacemaker.

Irenaeus is known for his defense of the Apostolic Tradition and his fidelity to the teachings transmitted through the Apostles and their successors, the bishops. His most noteworthy work is The Detection and Overthrow of the Gnosis Falsely So-Called (Adversus Haereses). *He died about A.D. 202.*

✤

It is within the power of all, therefore, in every Church, who may wish to see the truth, to contemplate clearly the tradition of the apostles manifested throughout the whole world; and we are in a position to reckon up those who were by the apostles instituted bishops in the

Churches, and the succession of these even to our own times; those who neither taught nor knew of anything like what these [heretics] rave about. For if the apostles had known hidden mysteries, which they were in the habit of imparting to "the perfect" apart and privately from the rest, they would have delivered them especially to those to whom they were also committing the Churches themselves. (*Adversus haereses III, III, 1, ANF I.*)

✤

... [W]e do put to confusion all those who ... assemble in unauthorized meetings ... by indicating that tradition derived from the apostles ... as also [by pointing out] the faith preached to men, which comes down to our times by means of the succession of the bishops. (*Adversus haereses III, III, 2, ANF I.*)

✤

... [I]t is incumbent to obey the presbyters who are in the Church — those who, as I have shown, possess the succession from the apostles; those who, together with the succession of the episcopate, have received the certain gift of truth, according to the good pleasure of the Father. (*Adversus haereses IV, XXVI, 2, ANF I.*)

Where, therefore, the gifts of the Lord have been placed, there it behoves us to learn the truth, [namely,] from those who possess that succession of the Church which is from the apostles, and among whom exists that which is sound and blameless in conduct, as well as that which is unadulterated and incorrupt in speech. (*Adversus haereses IV, XXVI, 5, ANF I.*)

6

Clement of Alexandria

Clement of Alexandria was a Christian teacher, philosopher, and director of the catechetical school in Alexandria about the year A.D. 200. He is recognized as the first Christian humanist, a moralist and a Christian "gnostic." He was a scholar who was convinced that true learning and the gospel belong together. He died between the years A.D. 211 and A.D. 216.

One of Clement's great works is the Stromateis, *a kind of early* Quaestiones disputatae. *In the following excerpt, we see the way in which he found spiritual meaning in all things.*

Even here in the Church, the gradations of bishops, presbyters and deacons happen to be imitations, in my opinion, of the angelic glory and of that arrangement which, the Scriptures say, awaits those who have followed in the footsteps of the Apostles, and who have lived in perfect righteousness according to the Gospel. (*Stromateis*, 6, 13, 107, 2, *The Faith of the Early Fathers*, Volume One.)

7

Hippolytus of Rome

St. Hippolytus was the first anti-pope during the time that St. Callistus was bishop of Rome. He was reconciled to the Church and died a martyr in A.D. 235. The Apostolic Tradition *is his earliest (A.D. 215), most important work. It provides valuable information on the liturgy and on the hierarchical organization of the early Church.*

Let the bishop be ordained after he has been chosen by all the people. When someone pleasing to all has been named, let the people assemble on the Lord's Day with the presbyters and with such bishops as may be present. All giving assent, the bishops shall impose hands on him, and the presbytery shall stand by in silence. Indeed, all shall remain silent, praying in their hearts for the descent of the Spirit. (*The Apostolic Tradition, 2, The Faith of the Early Fathers*, Volume One.)

The bishop shall give thanks as we have prescribed. Certainly, it is not necessary for him to recite the exact words which we have set down, by learning to say them from memory in his giving thanks to God. Rather, let each one pray according to his ability. Indeed, if he is able to pray in an accomplished manner and with a lofty style of prayer, it is well. But even if he has only a moderate ability in praying and in giving praise, let no one forbid it, so long as his prayer is of sound faith. (*The Apostolic Tradition, 10, The Faith of the Early Fathers*, Volume One.)

But none will refute these [errors], save the Holy Spirit bequeathed unto the Church, which the Apostles, having in the first instance received, have transmitted to those who have rightly believed. But we, as being their successors, and as participators in this grace, high-priesthood, and office of teaching, as well as being reputed guardians of the Church, must not be found deficient in vigilance, or disposed to suppress correct doctrine. (*The Refutation of All Heresies*, I, *The Proemium, ANF V.*)

8

Origen

Origen, successor to Clement as director of the theological school of Alexandria, has been recognized as the "greatest scholar of Christian antiquity." He was, certainly, the most outstanding Christian scholar, teacher, and theologian before Augustine. The heterodox character of some of his doctrines and the misrepresentation of others, after his death, have led many to regard him as a heretic. Jean Danielou's study, Origen, *has led to a reexamination and reassessment of the contribution of this great writer.*

And I think that those who faithfully discharge the office of a bishop in the Church may fitly be called the rafters, by which the whole building is sustained and protected, both from the rain and from the heat of the sun. . . . Moreover, the rafters are said to be of cypress, which tree possesses a greater strength and a sweetness of smell; and that denotes a bishop as being at once sound in good works and fragrant with the grace of teaching. (*Commentary on the Song of Songs, III, 3, ACW 26.*)

9

Cyprian of Carthage

Caecilius Cyprianus was bishop of Carthage in Northern Africa (A.D. 249 — A.D. 258). He was a great admirer of Tertullian. He guided his church through a severe persecution and died, himself, a martyr in a second attack against the Church in Africa during his episcopacy.

The following texts reveal his concern for the vigor and unity of the Church and his conviction that the bishop is to contribute to this life in its oneness and vitality.

Now this oneness we must hold to firmly and insist on —especially we who are bishops and exercise authority in the Church — so as to demonstrate that the episcopal power is one and undivided too. Let none mislead the brethren with a lie, let none corrupt the true content of the faith by a faithless perversion of the truth. The authority of the bishops forms a unity, of which each holds his part in its totality. (*On the Unity of the Catholic Church, 5, ACW 25.*)

✤

Does a man think he is with Christ when he acts in opposition to the bishops of Christ, when he cuts himself off from the society of His clergy and people? He is bearing arms against the Church, he is waging war upon God's institution. (*On the Unity of the Catholic Church, 17, ACW 25.*)

✤

Therefore, the duty of a bishop of the Lord is, not to deceive with false flatteries, but to provide the remedies needed for salvation. (*On the Lapsed, 14, ACW 25.*)

✤

For in proportion as the fall of a bishop is an event which tends ruinously to the fall of his followers, so on the other hand it is a useful and helpful thing when a bishop, by the firmness of his faith, sets himself forth to his brethren as an object of imitation. (*Epistle III, 1, ANCL, VIII.*)

✤

Let them not think that the way of life or salvation exists for them if they have refused to obey the bishops and priests since the Lord God says in Deuteronomy: "And any man who has the insolence to refuse to listen to the priest or judge, whoever he may be in those days, that man shall die.... And all the people, on hearing of it, shall fear and never again be so insolent." (*Epistle 4, 4, FOTC 51.*)

The Divine Protection will accomplish that we ... may keep in the harmonious unanimity of the Catholic Church, so that the Lord who condescends to elect and to appoint for Himself bishops in His Church, may protect those chosen and also appointed by His will and assistance, inspiring them in their government and supplying both vigor for restraining the insolence of the wicked and mildness for nourishing the repentance of the lapsed. (*Letter 48, 4, FOTC 51.*)

While the bond of concord remains, and the undivided sacrament of the Catholic Church endures, every bishop disposes and directs his own acts, and will have to give an account of his purposes to the Lord. (*Epistle LI, 21, ANF V.*)

But deacons ought to remember that the Lord chose apostles, that is, bishops and overseers;

while apostles appointed for themselves dea-cons after the ascent of the Lord into heaven, as ministers of their episcopacy and of the Church. (*Epistle LXIV, 3 ANF V.*)

For as the ruin of a leader is a dangerous incen-tive to the lapse of his followers, so, on the other hand, is it useful and salutary when a bishop shows himself to the brethren as one to be imitated in the strength of faith. (*Letter 9, 1, FOTC 51.*)

(*Moses et al, to Cyprian*) For to whom rather ought we to entrust our petition that he entreat for us than to such a glorious bishop...? (*Letter 31, 5, FOTC 51.*)

Our Lord, whose precepts we ought to fear and to keep, assigning the honor of the bishop and the plan for His Church, speaks in the Gospel and says to Peter: "I say to thee that thou art Peter, and upon this rock I will build my Church, and the gates of hell shall not prevail against it. And I will give thee the keys of the kingdom of heaven; and whatever thou shalt bind on earth shall be bound also in heaven, and whatever thou shalt loose on earth, shall be loosed also in heaven." (*Letter 33, 1, FOTC 51.*)

31

From that time the ordination of bishops and the plan of the Church flows on through the changes of times and successions; for the Church is founded upon the bishops, and every act of the Church is controlled by these same rulers. Since this has indeed been established by divine law, I marvel at the rash boldness of certain persons who have desired to write to me as if they were writing their letters in the name of the Church, since the Church is established upon the bishop and upon the clergy and upon all who stand firm in the faith. (*Letter 33 (27)*, *1, Faith of the Early Fathers*, Volume One.)

(*Priests and Deacons of Rome to Cyprian*) It is time ... that they should draw divine mercy upon themselves by due honor to the bishop of God. (*Letter 36, 3, FOTC 51.*)

Continue frequently in your prayers and aid our entreaties with your entreaties, that the mercy of God, favoring us may quickly return the bishop unharmed to his people.... (*Letter 38, 2, FOTC 51.*)

But ... This was the cause of his remaining: that the Lord might ... adorn with glorious bishops the number of our priests.... (*Letter 40, FOTC 51.*)

... [T]he bishop ought to provide for peace and tranquility in all things.... (*Letter 43, 4, FOTC 51.*)

... [T]here is ... also one episcopate diffused in a harmonious multitude of many bishops.... (*Letter 55, 24, FOTC 51.*)

We have learned, dearly beloved Brother, the glorious testimonies of your faith and virtue and we have received the honor of your confession so exultingly that we think ourselves also sharers and allies in your merits and praises. For, since we have one Church and a united mind and indivisible concord, what bishop does not exult in the praises of his fellow bishop as if they were his own or what brotherhood everywhere does not rejoice in the joy of its brethren?

While you are so unanimous, while you are brave, you have given great examples of unity and strength to the rest of the brethren. You have taught mightily to fear God, firmly to adhere to Christ; you have taught the people to be joined to their bishops in danger, brethren not to be separated from brethren in persecution, that a united harmony not only can in no way be overcome, but, at the same time, whatever is asked by all, the God of peace grants to peacemakers. (*Letter 60, 1 and 2, FOTC 51.*)

...[T]hat there may attend the altar of God a bishop who exhorts his people, not by words but by deeds, to undertake the arms of confession ... and ... prepares soldiers for battle, not alone by the incitement of his voice and words, but by the example of his faith and virtue. (*Letter 61, 2, FOTC 51.*)

For if we are bishops of God and of Christ, I do not find anyone we ought to follow more than God and Christ since He Himself in His Gospel emphatically says: "I am the light of the world. He who follows me will not walk in the darkness, but will have the light of life." (*Letter 63, 18, FOTC 51.*)

...[Y]et the Church does not withdraw from Christ, and the people united to their bishop and the flock clinging to their shepherd are the Church. (*Letter 66, 8, FOTC 51.*)

... [Y]ou ought to know that the bishop is in the Church and the Church is in the bishop and, if there is anyone who is not with the bishop, he is not in the Church. (*Letter 66, 8, FOTC 51.*)

...[I]n vain, they flatter themselves who creep up not having peace with the priests of God and they believe they are in communion secretly with certain ones when the Church which is one, Catholic, is not divided nor rent, but is certainly united and joined, in turn, by the solder of the bishops adhering to one another. (*Letter 66, 8, FOTC 51.*)

For that reason, therefore, dearly beloved Brother, is the large body of bishops joined by the bond of mutual concord and the chain of unity so that, if anyone of our college should attempt to engage in heresy and wound and lay waste the flock of Christ, the others, as useful and merciful shepherds, should assist and should assemble the sheep of the Lord into the flock. (*Letter 68, 3, FOTC 51.*)

For although we shepherds are many, yet we feed one flock.... (*Letter 68, 4, FOTC 51.*)

35

... [N]or can he be counted as a bishop, who, succeeding to no one and despising evangelical and apostolic tradition, has sprung from himself. For he who was not ordained in the Church can neither have nor keep the Church in any way. (*Letter 69, 3, FOTC 51.*)

... [E]very prelate, who will render an account of his actions to the Lord, should decide what he thinks best, according to what the blessed Apostle Paul writes in his Epistle to the Romans and says: "Every one of us will render an account for himself. Therefore, let us not judge one another." (*Letter 69, 17, FOTC 51.*)

For bishops and ministers who serve the altar and the sacrifices ought to be upright and unstained.... (*Letter 72, 2, FOTC 51.*)

... [T]he blessed Apostle Paul writes to Timothy and warns that the bishop ought not to be quarrelsome, or contentious, but gentle and teachable. But he who is meek and mild in the patience of learning is teachable. For bishops ought not only to teach, but also to learn because he who grows daily and profits by learning better things teaches better. (*Letter 74, 10, FOTC 51.*)

... [I]t is fitting for a bishop to confess the Lord there in that city in which he presides over the Church of the Lord and to glorify the whole people by the confession of their leader in their presence. (Letter 81, FOTC 51.)

For neither does anyone of us set himself up as a bishop, nor by tyranny and terror does anyone compel his colleagues to the necessity of obedience, since every bishop has his own free will to the unrestrained exercise of his liberty and power, so that neither can he be judged by another, nor is he himself able to judge another. Rather, let us all await the judgment of our Lord Jesus Christ, the one and only one who has both the power of setting us over the governing of His Church, and of judging our conduct in that capacity. (Acts of the Seventh Council of Carthage, (A.D. 256) Cyprian Presiding; *Proem., The Faith of the Early Fathers*, Volume One.)

Constitutions of the Holy Apostles

This work, also known as the Apostolic Constitutions, *contains legislative and liturgical material dating from about the beginning of the end of the fourth century, although it claims the authorship of Clement of Rome (+ c. A.D. 100). The Quinisext Council (Trullan Synod, A.D. 692) condemned the work, with the exception of book eight, chapter forty-seven, for being "falsified by heretics."*

But concerning bishops, we have heard from our Lord, that a pastor who is to be ordained a bishop for the churches in every parish, must be unblameable, unreprovable, free from all kinds of wickedness common among men.... (*II, I, I, ANF VIII.*)

Let him therefore be sober, prudent, decent, firm, stable, not given to wine; no striker, but gentle; not a brawler, not covetous.... (*II, I, II, ANF VII.*)

Let him also be merciful, of a generous and loving temper.... Let him be also ready to give, a lover of the widow and the stranger; ready to serve, and minister, and attend; resolute in his duty; and let him know who is the most worthy of his assistance. (*II, II III, ANF VII.*)

A bishop must be no accepter of persons; neither revering nor flattering a rich man contrary to what is right, nor overlooking nor domineering over a poor man.... Let a bishop be frugal, and contented with a little in his meat and drink, that he may be ever in a sober frame, and disposed to instruct and admonish the ignorant; and let him not be costly in his diet, a pamperer of himself, given to pleasure or fond of delicacies. Let him be patient and gentle in his admonitions, well instructed himself, meditating in and diligently studying the Lord's books, and reading them frequently, that so he may be able carefully to interpret the Scriptures, expounding the Gospel in correspondence with the prophets and with the law; and let the expositions from the law and the prophets correspond to the Gospel. (*II, II, V, ANF VII.*)

Hilary of Poitiers

St. Hilary, bishop of Poitiers in France, is one of the Doctors of the Church. Although he did not attend the Council of Nicaea (A.D. 325), he is known as "the Athanasius of the West," because of his defense of the Nicene teaching, against the Arians. His best known work is a treatise on the Trinity, De Trinitate.

The statement of the Apostle [cf. Titus 1:9-10] ... represents the perfect ruler of the Church with the perfect goods of the highest virtues so that his life might be adorned by his learning and his learning by his life. (*De Trinitate 8, 1, FOTC 25.*)

12

Saint Ambrose

Ambrose was chosen bishop of Milan while still a catechumen and was consecrated one week after he had been baptized. He was an exemplary spiritual leader and has left to the heritage of Christian literature dogmatic, scriptural, moral and ascetical writings as well as a collection of hymns. His struggles in favor of the liberty of the Church helped to clarify State-Church relations in the fourth century and set firm principles for the future.

But if we examine the context of holy Scripture or of times past, who will deny that in a matter of faith, in a matter, I say, of faith, bishops usually judge Christian emperors, not emperors, bishops. (*Letter to Valentinian, 21, FOTC 26.*)

And there is nothing in a bishop so fraught with danger before God, so base before men, as not

41

to declare freely what he thinks. Who will dare tell you the truth if the bishop does not? (*Letters to Emperors, 40, FOTC 26.*)

Now, where is the Church, save where the bishop's staff flourishes (cf. Num 17:23) and his charism? Often she is there, so that she may be put to the proof in bitterness and temptation. *(Isaac. or the Soul, 8, 64, FOTC 65.)*

Saint Jerome

St. Jerome is one of the Latin Fathers of the Golden Age of patristic literature. He was a priest and a scholar, devoting much of his life to study and translation of the Bible into Latin. Jerome's writings are frequently marked by satire and sharp castigations. His love of the Church and her Scriptures are beyond doubt.

❧

Not all bishops are bishops. . . . Let every man prove himself and so draw near. Ecclesiastical rank does not make a Christian. (*Letter 14, ACW 33.*)

❧

There is no man, I say, or only a few, who have all of the virtues that are required of a bishop. And yet, if any bishop lacks one or two of the virtues that have been listed (cf. 1 Tim. 3: 2-4), he will not, therefore, be deprived of the title of just, nor will he be condemned for what he does not have, but rather will be crowned for what he does possess. (*Against the Pelagians (22), FOTC 53.*)

Let no one, therefore, say: I am a bishop; I am a priest, or a deacon or a monk; I am a prince in this world. God is powerful enough to destroy the spirit of princes. (*Homily 9 on Psalm 75 (76), FOTC 48.*)

"My eyes are upon the faithful of the land, that they may dwell with me." The psalmist did not say upon the rich, or upon emperors, or bishops, or priests, or deacons, but upon the faithful; with them I will abide. A bishop who is a holy man has a right to these words.... (*Homily 27 on Psalm 100 (101), FOTC 48.*)

14

Saint Augustine of Hippo

St. Augustine has often been called "the greatest doctor of the Church." Surely, before Thomas Aquinas, no other Christian thinker has rivalled the theological and scholarly achievements of this great bishop and saint. His teachings on the episcopacy are reenforced by the strength of his own example as a spiritual leader in the Church.

... [F]or the title, *bishop*, signifies one who superintends, one who takes care of others by watching over them. (*Sermon 94, "The Slothful Servant," FOTC 11.*)

For this reason, overseers (*epískopoi*) or rulers are set over the churches, to reprimand sin, not to spare it. (*The City of God, Bk. 1, FOTC 8.*)

... [T]he office of bishop, *episcopatus*, implies work rather than dignity. The word is derived from *episkopos*, which is Greek for "superintendent." Thus, a bishop is supposed to superintend those over whom he is set in the sense that he is to "oversee" or "look out for" those under him. The word, *skopeia*, like the Latin *intendere*, means to look, and so *episkopein*, like *superintendere*, means "to oversee" or "to look out for those who are under one." Thus, no man can be a good bishop if he loves his title but not his task. (*The City of God, Bk. XIX, FOTC 24.*)

These are the bad nets which fishermen ought especially guard against, if in that parable fishers are to be understood as bishops or superiors of a lower order in the Church, because of the words: "Come, and I will make you fishers of men."

With good nets can be caught fish good and bad: with bad nets, however, good fish cannot be caught since from good teaching one can be good — he who hears and heeds — and another can be bad — he who hears and does not heed, but from bad doctrine he who thinks that the teaching is true although he does not submit to it is bad and he who submits is worse. (*Faith and Works* (*De fide et operibus*) *Chapter 17, 32, FOTC 27.*)

Palladius

Little is known of Palladius, a fourth-century monk. About the year A.D. 400, he became a bishop and was known as a supporter and admirer of St. John Chrysostom. The Lausiac History, *along with the* Life of St. Antony *by St. Athanasius, is one of the extant sources for the history of early monasticism in Egypt.*

As bishop you would have to be ordained and labor much and suffer many tribulations. (*The Lausiac History 35, 11, ACW 34.*)

16

Saint Leo the Great

St. Leo the Great is the greatest pope in early Christianity. He brought to the Church of Rome a high quality of spiritual leadership, and he bequeathed to the entire world of catholic Christianity a clarification of christological doctrine and a treasury of homilies and instructions, which can still be appreciated today.

Although it is proper that all those who are consecrated bishops be approved of and pleasing to God, we desire even superior excellence in those who we know are going to be in charge of fellow bishops under their jurisdiction. (*Letter 6, FOTC 34.*)

17

Julianus Pomerius

Pomerius, a priest and rhetor of the fifth century, is known as the teacher of Caesarius, later saint and bishop of Arles, in Gaul. His work, De vita contemplativa, *was written at the request of a bishop and expresses the ideals of the contemplative and the active life. The first half of the work is addressed to bishops.*

... [F]reedom from all occupations of the world and the study of Sacred Scripture — bishops can have even here; but those who on separating themselves from all the entanglements of world affairs do not grow sluggish in idleness but pursue the business of their perfection and who, turning from the folly of worldly wisdom, untiringly devote themselves to the Word of God, become truly wise, have knowledge of heavenly matters, despise worldly affairs, refute the opponents of sound doctrine, instruct the obedient, apply themselves to holy virtues by which they may each day become closer to God, and, eager for their own improvement as well as for that of all their disciples, receive even here some taste, as it were, of the contemplative life, whereby they are more keenly stimulated to it. ... Accordingly, they are not made vain because here they are honored as leaders of all faithful Catholics; but they rejoice rather that there they will be more distinguished members of Christ, who is the Head of priests and of all the faithful.

Only those attain it [the contemplative life] who have made effort to be what they have become; who strive not to seem, but to be what they are; who are distinguished not by the praise of others but by their own conduct, conspicuous not only because of their own rank but more because of the nobility of their priestly life; who are bishops not by title only but by virtue — men fit for the contemplative life, and coheirs of the joys of heaven. (*The Contemplative Life, I, ACW 4.*)

18

Saint Caesarius of Arles

St. Caesarius is known as a tireless pastor who brought to an end the semi-Pelagian controversies which raged in the early sixth century. However, Caesarius was more concerned about moral teaching than about theological speculation. He was one of the principal participants at the Second Council of Orange. His convictions about the necessity of good preaching led him to recommend a practice which he did not hesitate to follow himself: when his own resources failed, he took up and used as his own sermons and homiletic material from the earlier Fathers of the Church.

Hence, bishops are said to be watchmen because they have been placed in a higher position, as if on the top of the citadel of the Church, and have been established on the altar, and so should be solicitous for the city and the field of God, that is, the entire Church, guarding not only the wide expanse of the gates, that is, by salutary preaching prohibiting serious sin, but also watching the rear doors and little rabbit-holes. In other words, they should continually advise the detection and cleansing of slight offenses which daily creep up, by means of fasting, alms, and prayer. (*Sermon 1, 4, FOTC 31.*)

With this kind of cultivation bishops should always be occupied. Many are found who can plant in order or till the fields, but few and rare are the people who can provide nourishment for souls. (*Sermon 1, 6, FOTC 31.*)

[I]f we carefully heed the lessons which are read at the consecration of bishops, we have a means of arousing ourselves to the greatest compunction. What Gospel text is it, except the one I mentioned a little while ago? "Peter, Peter," it says, "feed my sheep," and again, "feed my sheep." Did Christ say: Cultivate the vineyards by your presence, arrange the country estates yourself, exercise the cultivation of land? He did not say this, but "Feed my sheep." Now, what kind of a prophetic text is read at the consecration of a bishop? It is this: "I have made thee a watchman to the house of Israel." It did not say a steward of vineyards or country estates, or the manager of fields; doubtless, it is a watchman of souls. (*Sermon 1, 11, FOTC, 31.*)

Perhaps someone will say: I am not eloquent, so I cannot explain anything concerning sacred Scripture. Even if this be true, God does not require of us what we are unable to do. So definite is it that this does not harm priests that, even if some possess worldly eloquence, there is no need of pontifical language, which scarcely reaches the understanding of even a few people. Can anyone not reveal or discuss with fitting eloquence obscure passages of the Old and New Testament and sound the depths of sacred Scripture? (*Sermon 1, 12,[1] FOTC, 31.*)

I do not know whether there is any bishop, presbyter, or even a deacon who cannot preach in church or advise everywhere these truths and many others like them. No eloquence or great memory is sought here where a simple admonition in ordinary language is understood to be necessary. If anyone takes away our earthly substance, we presume to bring in the most

---

[1]This entire sermon is instructive for the teaching a bishop is encouraged to do through his own study and knowledge of the gospel.

powerful judges and scholars of rhetoric to intervene with the highest authority, so that we may be able to recover our material possessions from the usurper. ... Why do we cry out for the land? Because we love the land. Why do we not shout in church? I have not dared to say it, but the truth compels me not to keep silent. We do not cry out in church because we do not love the people entrusted to our care. (*Sermon 1, 13, FOTC 31.*)

[W]e are called shepherds, pilots, and bishops. If we truly are shepherds, we ought to provide spiritual pastures for the Lord's flock. If we are pilots, we should with God's help direct the ship of the Church in the midst of the waves of this life, vigorously and courageously, so that without any error we may be able to enter the port of paradise in a straight course, after all the waves and storms. Now, a bishop is interpreted as an inspector on a lofty site. Therefore, since we have been placed in a higher position, let us with the Lord's help and great diligence fulfill the obligations of our title and always be solicitous for the Lord's sheep.... (*Sermon 1, 19, FOTC 31.*)

[L]et us not reserve ourselves for a repentance which is accepted at the end of life, but as long as we live let us endeavor to do penance daily. ... Indeed, a bishop who does penance every day can pray for me, but one who presumes upon his dignity and sanctity, refusing to do penance, will have to find someone to pray for him. (*Sermon 61, 1, FOTC 31.*)

What those proud Levites suffered because they assumed the priesthood without the Lord's command cf. Num 16: 36-40, will also be endured by men who attempt to install themselves in the office of bishop, priest, or deacon by means of bribes or flattery. Just as the former men were destroyed physically, so the latter are consumed in heart. (*Sermon 110, 1, FOTC 47.*)

It is not going to be said: Because you committed murder, because you committed adultery, because you seized the property of another, but only this are they going to hear: "For I was hungry, and you did not give me to eat." ... Now among those who will be sent to the left hand will not only be the laity, but also many bishops, and what is worse, wicked clerics, even avaricious or proud monks, as well as angry, haughty or covetous religious and widows. If fruitful repentance does not come to their assistance, they are going to hear that dreadful, irrevocable sentence: "Depart from me, accursed ones, into the everlasting fire." (*Sermon 157, 4, FOTC 47.*)

Among other precepts of his the blessed Apostle also says this, that a bishop should be strong in rebuking objectors with sound doctrine. It is a great work, but a heavy burden. ... There is no reason which makes the dispenser of God slothful in rebuking objectors more than fear of a harsh word. For as long as we fear the calumny, ridicule, and reproaches of proud men and fear to be burdened by them with respect to earthly possessions, when we are afraid of losing temporal goods, we preach eternal ones less than we should. As long as we dread to lose something worldly through the wickedness of such men, we neglect to take care of the wounds of their sins with spiritual remedies. (*Sermon 183, 2, FOTC 47.*)

To enlighten the human race, beloved ..., our Lord lit many spiritual lamps in this world. ... What, however, are these lamps, which our Lord permitted to dispel and illuminate the fog of faithlessness? First the patriarchs, then the prophets, afterwards the apostles, and finally the bishops of all the churches. (*Sermon 214, 1, FOTC 66.*)

Many times even doctors of the Church are wont to stop rebuking sinners, not through carelessness but because they are afraid that the sinners will rush out to worse crimes as a result of the reproof. When bishops fail to preach for this reason, they cannot be guilty because of their silence. (*Sermon 217, 3, FOTC 66.*)

The office of bishop is a good work ... as the blessed Apostle says: "Whoever wants to be a bishop aspires to a noble task." Now when "task" is heard, labor is understood. Therefore whoever desires the office of bishop with this understanding, wants it without the arrogance of ambition. To express this more clearly, if a man wants not so much to be in authority over the people of God as to help them, he aspires to be a bishop in the true spirit. (*Sermon 230, 1, FOTC 66.*)

[I]t redounds to the honor and advantage of all the faithful, when they have such a bishop, by whose assistance many people are helped and by whose example they are inspired. .... For this reason, dearest brother, I advise you with a unique and singular charity, that authority may not be lacking to your humility, that gentleness may affect your firmness, mildness temper your justice, and patience restrain your freedom of action. Avoid pride, into which it is natural for anyone to fall, and pursue humility, in which everyone ought to grow. Let your beloved self not be ignorant of the laws of the Church, in order that you may keep the rights of your authority within the rules and regulations of the Fathers. To be sure it is said "that the law is not aimed at the good man," because he fulfills the norm of the precept by the judgment of his will. True love holds within itself both the authority of the Apostles and canonical sanctions, and let your pious will always pursue examples of these. (*Sermon 230, 2, FOTC 66.*)

[W]ith the Lord's help courageously cling to patience in great fear and trembling. In addition, if grief and trouble, even perils and reproaches from an unlearned people are stirred up as the result of a spirit of animosity, bear them with courage and constancy. Look rather to our Lord and Savior, the true shepherd who condescended to suffer, not only tribulation but even death, for the sake of His

sheep. It is necessary for you to bear many adversities, if you want to preserve right doctrine and continuously to preach the Word of God as it is expedient to do. (*Sermon 230, 4, FOTC 66.*)

Mark and see to it that involvement in worldly affairs not keep you so occupied that you are unable to have time for the Word of God. ... Christ did not appoint you to be the cultivator of fields but to be the shepherd of souls. ... [A]ssume the office of preaching in such a way that you may not be unable to have time for the Word of God and to provide the spiritual food of souls to your flock because you are choked by present cares. (*Sermon 230, 5, FOTC 66.*)

[L]et us pray, dearly beloved, that my episcopacy may be profitable for both you and me. It will be useful to me if I preach what should be done; it will be advantageous for you if you practice what you have heard. If we ceaselessly pray for you with the perfect love of charity and you do the same for us, with the Lord's help we will happily reach eternal bliss. May He deign to grant this, who lives and reigns for ever and ever. Amen. (*Sermon 232, 4, FOTC 66.*)

BIBLIOGRAPHY OF WORKS CONSULTED

ANCIENT CHRISTIAN WRITERS. Johannes Quasten, S.T.D. and Joseph C. Plumpe, Ph.D., editors. Westminster, Maryland: The Newman Bookshop (unless otherwise indicated).

Volume 1.   James A. Kleist, S.J., Ph.D. (trans.); 1946.

Volume 4.   Sister Mary Josephine Suelzer, Ph.D. (trans.); 1947.

Volume 6.   James A. Kleist, S.J., Ph.D. (trans.); 1948.

Volume 25.   Maurice Bévenot, S.J. (trans., ann.); Westminster, Maryland: The Newman Press; 1957.

Volume 26.   R.P. Lawson (trans.); New York, New York/Ramsey, New Jersey: Newman Press; 1956.

Volume 33.   Charles C. Mierow, Ph.D. (trans) and Thomas C. Lawler (intro. and notes); Westminster, Maryland: The Newman Press; 1963.

Volume 34.　Robert T. Meyer, Ph.D. (trans., ann.); Westminster, Maryland: The Newman Press: 1965.

ANTE-NICENE CHRISTIAN LIBRARY. Rev. Alexander Roberts, D.D., and James Donaldson, LL.D., editors. Edinburgh: T. & T. Clark; MDCCCLXVIII.

Volume VIII.　Rev. Robert E. Wallis, Ph.D. (trans.); MDCCCLXVIII.

ANTE-NICENE FATHERS. The Rev. Alexander Roberts, D.D., and James Donaldson, LL.D., editors. American reprint of the Edinburgh edition. New York: Charles Scribner's Sons.

Volume I.　A. Cleveland Coxe, D.D., (arr.); 1925.

Volume V.　A. Cleveland Coxe, D.D., (arr.); 1919.

THE FATHERS OF THE CHURCH. Roy Joseph Deferrari, et al., editorial board. Washington, D.C.: The Catholic University of America Press (unless otherwise indicated).

Volume 8.　Demetrius B. Zema, S.J. and Gerald G. Walsh, S.J. (trans.); New York: Fathers of the Church, Inc.; 1950.

Volume 11.　Denis J. Kavanagh, O.S.A. (trans); New York: Fathers of the Church, Inc.; 1951.

Volume 24. Gerald G. Walsh, S.J. and Daniel J. Honan (trans.): New York: Fathers of the Church, Inc.; 1954.

Volume 25. Stephen McKenna, C.SS.R. (trans.); New York: Fathers of the Church, Inc.; 1954.

Volume 26. Sister Mary Melchior Beyenka, O.P. (trans.): New York: Fathers of the Church, Inc.; 1954.

Volume 27. Sister Mary Liguori, I.H.M., Ph.D. (trans.); New York: Fathers of the Church, Inc.; 1955.

Volume 31. Sister Mary Magdeleine Mueller, O.S.F. (trans.): New York: Fathers of the Church, Inc.; 1956.

Volume 34. Brother Edmund Hunt, C.S.C. (trans.); New York: Fathers of the Church, Inc.; 1957.

Volume 38. Sister Mary Sarah Muldowney, R.S.M. (trans.); New York: Fathers of the Church, Inc.; 1959.

Volume 47. Sister Mary Magdeleine Mueller, O.S.F. (trans.); 1964.

Volume 48. Sister Marie Liguori Ewald, I.H.M. (trans.): 1964.

Volume 51. Sister Rose Bernard Donna, C.S.J. (trans.); 1964.

Volume 53. John N. Hritzer, Ph.D. (trans.); 1965.

Volume 65. Michael P. McHugh (trans.); Washington, D.C.: The Catholic University of America Press in association with Consortium Press; 1972.

Volume 66.   Sister Mary Magdeleine Mueller, O.S.F. (trans.); Washington, D.C.: The Catholic University of America Press in association with Consortium Press; 1973.

The Faith of the Early Fathers, Volume One. William A. Jurgens (trans.) Collegeville, Minnesota: The Liturgical Press; 1970.